A Woman With a Past, A God With a Future

Embracing God's Transforming Love

Elsa Kok

new
hope
PUBLISHERS

Birmingham, Alabama

New Hope® Publishers
P. O. Box 12065
Birmingham, AL 35202-2065
www.newhopepublishers.com

Library of Congress Cataloging-in-Publication Data

Kok, Elsa, 1968-
  A woman with a past, a God with a future : embracing God's transforming love / by Elsa Kok.
   p. cm.
  ISBN 1-59669-001-1 (softcover)
  1. Christian women—Religious life. 2. Bible—Study and teaching. I. Title.

  BV4527.K64 2006
  248.8'43—dc22
            2005037934

ISBN: 1-59669-001-1

N064128 • 0806 • 3M1

DEDICATION

I would like to dedicate this book to my family:

Brian, Sam, Sean, Jessica, and Cassie.

From my past, to a future with you . . .
I stand amazed and grateful!

TABLE OF CONTENTS

Acknowledgments

- *Brian:* I love you. Your steadfast faith and tender love melt my heart every day. I am a better follower of Christ because you reflect Him so well. Thank you.

- *Sam:* I love watching your story unfold. You are God's treasure and my delight. Life with you is a joy. I love you!

- *Sean:* I'm so glad you are in my life. I love you and believe in your future. I'm proud to call you son.

- *Jessica and Cassie:* You are loved beyond words. We think of you and pray for you (with tenderness and hope) every day.

- *Mom and Dad:* Thank you for being such sweet encouragers and wonderful friends. I truly delight in our relationship!

- *Jennifer:* As always, thank you for holding me fast, praying for me, and standing with me. You are a faithful friend. I love you.

- *Lissa:* You are a dear friend. Thanks for going to the deep places with me.

- *Piet, Carol, Enno, Rob, Laura, John and Wendy:* I love my family!

- *Andrea, Jan, Susan (and the periodicals team at Focus):* I learned so much from you. But even better, I loved every minute of it. You are gifts in my life. Thank you.

- *New Hope:* Thanks for believing in me, and for publishing books for women who long to know healing.

- *Reeses:* Another book has been written as you curled around my feet. I hope you live a long time. We have more books to write!

INTRODUCTION

Friend,

I wonder why you opened to this page. Maybe the title of the book caught your eye. Maybe, like me, your past has robbed you of too much future, and you're tired of it. You've come to the right place. This is not a Bible study that will preach to you, shame you, or condemn you. It's a journey—one that I'm still walking. It's a journey towards the truth about God and the wonderful things He has in mind for your future.

For me, Christianity was always hard to grasp. The Christians I knew were so squeaky clean there was no way I could measure up. I didn't think I could ever be like them— and honestly, I wasn't sure I wanted to try. Their world seemed boring to me. I was caught up in the things

that I wanted to do and many of those choices fell outside of what Christianity looked like. So I stayed far away. Although I'd grown up in the church, my relationship with God was very low on my priority list.

Then things began to change. As much as I hated to admit it, the "fun life" I was clinging to wasn't holding up very well. I went through a divorce. Soon after, I got a job at a bar, but I could barely pay the bills. I tried to find solace in other relationships, only to get my heart broken. I was addicted to cigarettes, and I had a tough time being honest with myself or anyone else. I was a mess. All my fun landed me in a life without any joy or hope.

It was amazing how God found me in that place. He brought people into my life who loved me just as I was. They showed me His heart, and as I began to experience their love, I imagined there might be a God who loved me too. I started checking things out—tentatively at first. But God paved the way. I started to seek Him. Instead of just believing what I'd been told, I wanted to know who God really was...and I found Him! The more I knew Him, the more I loved Him. There were dark times—especially when I would stumble headlong into an old habit, or I'd forget the depth of His love, or life would sideswipe me with a hard circumstance. I still grew—sometimes two steps forward, sometimes one step back. He never gave up on me.

I figured that God wanted me to forget about my past—that He wanted me to stick it underneath the rug and not embarrass Him by bringing it up.

I'm not sure where I got that idea. Maybe the way people seemed so good sitting in those church pews made me think they wouldn't want to know where I had been. But God changed that in my world. As I began to really love Him and have relationship with Him, He began to use my past in amazing ways. I would run into another woman who was hurting, and I would have the chance to share what I'd been through. All the stuff I did, which I thought disqualified me, ended up giving me the chance to help others in their hurt. That was an amazing thing! The more I grew in my faith, the more God turned those dark, broken pieces into something worthwhile and beautiful.

God has something wonderful in store for you too. Maybe you've done some wrong or questionable things—and you are ashamed. Maybe there is stuff in your life that you've never told anyone. Maybe you're not even sure about this whole God thing, and you doubt whether He really accepts you just as you are. It may sound nice and spiritual, but you may wonder, How can it possibly be true?

If that's the case, this book is for you. If you are hiding pieces of your story, if you feel disqualified in any way, if you wonder if God is tired of you, read on. Don't hide. It might be tough to dig around in your story, but it's worth it. Keep going, even when it feels too hard. Discover what His Word, the Bible, says about you and your circumstances. Learn to apply His truth in very personal ways. Look at your story and let the shame wash away. It's amazing to be released from the weight of our past. And God has that for you, I promise. Even better, He promises!

I would like to encourage you to work through this book with a friend, pastor, or small group. You need to see God's love "with skin on," as they say. There will be moments you will need a set of tender eyes to encourage you when you're stumbling through your story. Make sure the person you choose is safe. Make sure she has an authentic relationship with Jesus. You'll be able to tell—it's in the smile, the understanding of Scripture, the feeling you get—the feeling that you could pour out those dark places and still be accepted. If you can't find someone right now, go ahead and get started. God will meet you. He wants to free you from the past and give you a future unlike anything you can begin to imagine. He is that good. He loves you that much. It's true.

I will be praying for you.

Elsa Kok

13

WEEK ONE

When History Reappears

Anna was devastated. She'd done it again. It seemed like every time she was stressed, that same old habit crept up and got the best of her. Anna put her head in her hands as a small sigh escaped her. How could this happen? She had become a Christian; she wasn't supposed to make this kind of mistake. After all, her friend told her that when she accepted Christ, everything would be different. She'd be a new woman, free from all that stuff from her past.

She knew that Christians made mistakes, but not the big, glaring ones she always seemed to make. And she was certain that when "they" did it, it was never intentional.

Maybe my Christianity didn't take, she thought to herself. Maybe I'm not really a believer and so it isn't working. She wondered if God was angry with her. After all, she'd made all those lousy choices in the past, and now she'd blown her one and only chance to get it right. It's not like she didn't know it was wrong. She knew…but she did it anyway. She hadn't cared at the time.

I'll never get this right, she thought. Why even bother?

What do you think?

Can you relate to what Anna experienced? Are there certain choices you continue to make that frustrate you? Write about it in the space below.

_____

_____

_____

_____

Do you find yourself ready to give up on Christianity? On God? Does it seem too overwhelming to get it all right? Share where you are today.

_____

_____

_____

_____

Let's read the Bible.

Paul was an amazing Christian. He was one of those guys who just drew people to God. He was commanding when he needed to be, but gentle when the moment called for it. He loved Jesus with all his heart. In fact, he wrote several books of the Bible. You could say that if anyone understood Christianity, it was Paul. Let's listen to what he says:

> "For what I do is not the good I want to do; no, the evil I do not want to do—this I keep on doing."
> —Romans 7:19

What does this verse mean for us?

First, it means you don't have to walk around with such a heavy weight on your shoulders all the time. This is a journey for every one of us. Not a single person gets it completely right. Paul was one of the greatest Christians of all time. He traveled to many different countries and changed lives with his passion for Jesus—he helped people see the truth. Yet he was still frustrated by the fact that he wasn't perfect.

The wonderful thing is (and thankfully, Paul knew this) God promises that He won't ever turn us away when we're sorry (Psalm 51:17).

Does that mean that we can plan to keep messing up on purpose? No! It's miserable to be stuck in those old patterns. It does mean you can know forgiveness, take your eyes off the action, and think about what might be underneath, so you really can move past it.

For example, I smoked cigarettes for a long time. Sometimes I would get so angry with myself because I would quit for a while and then go back to it. I would focus on the cigarette smoking, and that's all I would think about. If I didn't smoke, I was a good girl. If I did, I was bad. I was on an emotional roller coaster, and it wiped me out! Then God began to teach me through friends and His Word, the Bible, that He didn't love me more or less because I smoked. He loved me just the same—but, of course, He wanted me free. As I understood that His love didn't change, it helped me to look at smoking without all that condemnation. So I started asking myself the why question: Why was I smoking? Did I smoke when I was scared? Lonely? Angry? Afraid? If so, what was making me scared or lonely or angry or afraid?

Those questions made me want to uncover my story. Stuff like smoking, broken relationships, and unhealthy thinking didn't just disappear when I became a Christian. God wasn't as concerned about the habits as He was about deeper things. He was concerned about the hurt underneath the habits. It was the hurt He wanted to heal. The stuff I was doing was a symptom of something deeper—and that's what He was after with His healing touch and incredible love.

How can we apply this truth?

Maybe Paul struggled with certain issues over and over because God wanted to teach him something specific about a weakness or wound in Paul's past. Maybe God wanted to remind him that He could meet Paul in that place. Do you think there might be bigger things beneath your habits and choices that God wants to show you? Write your thoughts.

_____

_____

_____

If you could accept that God loves you and wants to heal you . . . if you could really experience that healing, would you be willing to open your story and any old wounds to Him and to others? Is there anything stopping you from doing that? Take a minute and ask God to help you in this process. You don't have to write anything that sounds all flowery, just write your heart and ask for help. He will answer.

_____

_____

_____

_____

Your love letter

I can remember not understanding Scripture very well. It scared me to imagine living by this old book written so long ago by men in a completely different culture and environment. What could they have to say to a broken girl so many centuries later? Then I met a woman who became a dear friend. She had a tremendous love for the Bible and all the words that God had poured out to her through its pages. Her passion was contagious, and I wanted to know more. I began to really look at the various verses, and she helped me to apply them to my world. I began to see the Bible wasn't an old book written by men trying to rob me of fun. I began to see it was a love letter crafted by my Savior who wanted to give me some very real glimpses of His compassion, mercy, hope, joy, encouragement, and wisdom . . . and that by

A Woman With a Past, A God With a Future

living and learning and loving God through its pages, life would change dramatically for me. And it did.

So throughout this Bible study, we will dig into God's love letter for you. We'll use this section to remind you of stories where God has met people like you and me. In some chapters, this section will dig into particular verses and explain different concepts and stories; in others, I'll ask you to do the digging. My prayer as we go through the next 12 weeks is threefold:

- That you will learn to look in the Bible for practical advice for the real-life situations you encounter
- That you will learn about God's passion for you and His hope for your future
- That you will learn how much He loves and cares about the details (good and bad) in your world

To start, let's take a look at a few Scriptures that might help you understand the importance of looking at your story. . . of asking God to show you things. You see, He knows it all: how you are wired, why you make the choices you do, and what hurts are hidden in your heart. He not only knows—He wants to heal those places.

"Search me, O God, and know my heart; test me
and know my anxious thoughts."
—Psalm 139:23

"O Lord, you have searched me
    and you know me.
You know when I sit and when I rise;
    you perceive my thoughts from afar.
You discern my going out and my lying down;
    you are familiar with all my ways.
Before a word is on my tongue
    you know it completely, O Lord.
You hem me in—behind and before;
    you have laid your hand upon me.
Such knowledge is too wonderful for me,
    too lofty for me to attain.
Where can I go from your Spirit?
    Where can I flee from your presence?
If I go up to the heavens, you are there;
    if I make my bed in the depths, you are there.
If I rise on the wings of the dawn,
    if I settle on the far side of the sea,

A Woman With a Past, A God With a Future

even there your hand will guide me,

    your right hand will hold me fast.

If I say, 'Surely the darkness will hide me

    and the light become night around me,'

even the darkness will not be dark to you;

    the night will shine like the day,

    for darkness is as light to you.

For you created my inmost being;

    you knit me together in my mother's womb.

I praise you because I am fearfully and

      wonderfully made;

    your works are wonderful,

    I know that full well."

—Psalm 139:1–14

"'But I will restore you to health and heal your wounds,' declares the Lord."

—Jeremiah 30:17

What do you think these verses say about God's desire to deal with the things that seem to control and drive you?

_____

_____

_____

_____

If God is willing and able to heal the broken places in your life, do you think you might be willing to expose your story before Him—and to others who are willing to help? Why or why not?

_____

_____

_____

_____

Journal time

I encourage you to get a journal. Have it open with pen in hand as you read God's Word. Allow God to speak to you regarding your particular life story. He is crazy about you; He wants to speak to you. He wants to walk through the hard things with you—there is nothing that will stop Him from loving you. If you listen for Him, He will talk to you.

Try looking at the following verse, and see what God might be saying to you.

"But when he, the Spirit of truth, comes, he will guide you into all truth. He will not speak on his own; he will speak only what he hears, and he will tell you what is yet to come."
—John 16:13

Write the verse in your journal; then answer these two questions:

- What does this say about God's character?
- What does this verse mean for my life?

Here are references for some more Scriptures. For these, go straight to the source—God's Word. Look up one reference every day over the next week, write the verse in your journal, and answer our two questions.

Romans 8:39

Isaiah 57:18

Deuteronomy 31:8

Isaiah 61:3

WEEK TWO

UNFOLDING YOUR STORY

Elissa looked up from the ground into the eyes of her friend Anna. She expected to see anger or disgust—maybe even pity. What she didn't expect to see was kindness. "Didn't you hear what I just shared with you?" she asked.

Anna nodded and leaned closer. "Yes. I heard every word."

Elissa shook her head, "But . . ."

Anna took Elissa's hand in her own. "Listen. I'm not sure what you thought I would say, but what I want to say is 'I'm sorry.'"

"You're sorry?" Elissa was confused.

"Yes, I'm sorry. I'm sorry you went through those things. I'm sorry for the hurt I see in your eyes. I'm sorry that happened to you. It was wrong. You were a little girl, Elissa. You should have been loved, cherished, and treasured. You weren't." Anna paused and took a deep breath. "So you did what any little girl would do. You decided you weren't lovable or beautiful, and you made lots of decisions based on that. But dear one, you are lovable. You are beautiful.

What happened was wrong." She waited for Elissa to really hear her. She repeated herself. "What happened was wrong. *You* are not wrong; *what happened* was wrong. Do you understand?"

Elissa couldn't hold back the tears. She'd never told anyone the details of her story. She just assumed whoever listened would turn away. They wouldn't care, or if they did, they would only think less of her. She never imagined someone might listen, understand, and even stand up for her. The smallest glimmer of hope stirred in her belly. Maybe she could be rid of the weight that always seemed to press in on her heart. Oh, how sweet that would be!

What do you think?

Can you relate to Elissa? Is there a story in your heart longing to be told? When you picked up this book, what part of your past were you thinking about? If you know the answer, jot it down. If you're uncertain what prompted you to pick up the book, move on to the next thought.

_____

_____

_____

Take a moment to ask God to show you what He wants to uncover right now. It may be a specific event or situation; it may be the way you felt about yourself without ever really understanding why. Write a prayer in the following space, asking Him to help you take these next steps. Ask Him to direct your thoughts, so that He can protect you from going places you may not need to go. You don't have to sound spiritual or have all the right words. Just write what is in your heart. Ask Him for His help—He is willing and able.

_____

_____

_____

_____

Now let's go back to your story. I'm going to ask you a few questions. Answer as honestly as you can. Don't think of any situation as too small or too big. No one walks through life without wounds, and a small hurt to one person can be life changing for another. This is your time . . . your study . . . your journey to healing. Don't think about what anyone else would say or think, and don't limit your answer. If you run out of room, open a notebook or journal and keep writing.

When you were a little girl, what were your dreams? Who did you want to grow up to become, and what did you think your life would look like? Be specific.

_____

_____

_____

_____

How did your life deviate from those little girl dreams? Again, be specific.

_____

_____

_____

_____

When you think of people who were part of your story, who were the heroes (maybe individuals who believed in you, or took the time to look out for you)? Write about them: their names, what they were like, and what they did for you.

_____

_____

_____

_____

Who were the villains? Who do you have the hardest time forgiving?

_____

_____

_____

_____

Have you made choices that you can't let go? Do you have a difficult time forgiving yourself? Write what is on your heart.

_____

_____

_____

_____

_____

Let's read the Bible.

Remember, this is not a time to beat yourself up or stir up pieces of your history without purpose. We are uncovering these things to bring them under the light of God's truth. We will start by addressing the whole of your story. In the coming chapters, we'll talk about some of the specifics.

Now, let's go to the truth:

> "Therefore, there is now no condemnation for those who are in Christ Jesus."
> —Romans 8:1

> "He [Jesus] welcomed them and spoke to them about the kingdom of God, and healed those who needed healing."
> —Luke 9:11

What do these verses mean for us?

If you are like I was, you may imagine God standing in the heavens with His arms crossed and His foot tapping in frustration. You wonder if He has had enough of you, and you imagine that the voice in your thoughts—the one that criticizes every move—is His voice. It is not. He is not wagging His finger in your face. It is quite the opposite. He is waiting for you with open arms. He welcomes you. He wants you to expose your story to His light, so He can heal you. He speaks kind words of encouragement and strength to you. He is good. He doesn't want any piece of your life to stay hidden in secrecy under the cover of darkness.

You may be on the flip side of the spectrum. Maybe you are angry with God and you don't understand why He has allowed certain things to happen to you. We will cover that more in the coming chapters, but know this today: He wants to heal you. He knows your anger, and He can meet you in that place, too.

How can we apply these truths?

Since you may be feeling a little raw after pouring out your story on paper, take the verses we just talked about and make them personal. That's right—change them into a personal statement from God, with your name attached. For example, I might write God's message to me from Romans 8:1 like this: "Elsa, there is no condemnation in Me. That means that because you are Mine, there is nothing you can say or do that will cause My voice to turn mean. That nasty voice in your head is not Mine. I don't condemn. I correct. I love. I encourage. I pursue. I don't condemn." Now you try. Make Romans 8:1 and Luke 9:11 personal.

_____

_____

_____

_____

_____

_____

_____

Your love letter

The Bible is full of stories of the broken hearted, the foolish, and the prideful. That's what makes it all so real. If this were a made-up religion or an old book put together by people wanting to promote their own made-up God, they never would have included the stories they did. Liars, adulterers, cheaters, and murderers are included throughout the pages of Scripture. There is no perfectly clean life in the whole bunch—except, of course, for Jesus.

Every story had one of two endings: Either the person came to God and uncovered their "stuff" so He could heal it, or they tucked it away and hoped no one would notice.

The second group chose to live in their brokenness, because they weren't willing to let God help. We will talk about one of those stories in the next chapter.

But you are choosing the first ending—you started by picking up this book. I applaud you for uncovering your story. What a courageous step that was! Please know that your ending includes healing, joy, and hope. Take comfort: Our God is no stranger to the messes we get ourselves into, and if you are willing, He can heal you.

Journal time

Here are several more verses. Over the next week, read one every day, and write what it means in connection with your life and story.

> "O LORD my God, I called to you for help and you healed me."
> —Psalm 30:2

Malachi 4:2

Romans 8:39

Psalm 130:7

Isaiah 40:31

WEEK THREE

ACCEPTING YOUR JOURNEY

Tamar couldn't seem to shake the despair. From the moment her eyes opened in the morning to the hours of tossing and turning before sleep, she battled hopelessness. She couldn't stop replaying it in her mind. It had been a quiet morning when word came that her brother Amnon was sick and her dad wanted her to go take care of him. She was a good cook and didn't mind helping out, so she had gone over to her brother's home and spent the morning preparing some fresh bread. She had kneaded the dough and then cleaned up around the house as it baked. When the bread was ready, she took it, fresh and warm, to her brother's bedside.

Tamar never expected the thing that happened next—she never saw it coming. Her brother had sent everyone away just moments earlier. Tamar thought he was probably tired and needed quiet. Instead, when she drew close, he reached up to take hold of her. Tamar was scared and tried to pull away, but her brother was stronger. She tried to reason with him, but he wouldn't hear it. He raped her.

Tamar shook her head, trying to shake off the memory, but she couldn't seem to stop it from replaying in her mind. She didn't dare tell anyone—she was too embarrassed, too full of shame. Her other brother, Absalom, figured out what happened and asked her about it. He opened his home to her, but it was tough for Absalom to understand all that she was feeling. He told her not to "take this thing to heart." But Tamar couldn't help it. After what happened, there seemed to be no hope left for her future. Who would want her now?

This story can be found in 2 Samuel 13.

What do you think?

Can you relate to what Tamar felt? Have you battled sleepless nights over someone's betrayal—whether sexual or nonsexual? Write about it (as much or as little as you feel comfortable writing). If you don't write it, I encourage you to talk with someone about it or share it in the safety of a small group.

_____

_____

_____

_____

_____

_____

_____

How do you think God felt about Tamar's situation? If you were someone who loved Tamar, how would you feel?

_____

_____

_____

_____

_____

How do you think God feels about the hurts you've experienced?

_____

_____

_____

_____

_____

Let's read the Bible.

"When Mary reached the place where Jesus was and saw him, she fell at his feet and said, 'Lord, if you had been here, my brother would not have died.' When Jesus saw her weeping, and the Jews who had come along with her also weeping, he was deeply moved in spirit and troubled. 'Where have you laid him?' he asked. 'Come and see, Lord,' they replied. Jesus wept."
—John 11:32–35

What do these verses mean for us?

Let me explain a little more of the story. Jesus came to His friends, who were heartbroken and sad because Lazarus, someone they loved, had died. But Jesus was more than able to help Lazarus. In fact, shortly thereafter, He did. He raised him from the dead. So here's the question: Why did Jesus cry?

I think Jesus cried because of the sadness of those He loved. The women came to Him, devastated because of their loss. He looked at their mournful faces, tears streaming down their cheeks, and His heart ached with theirs. Even though He knew He was going to perform a miracle and bring life from death in just a few moments, He still wept. I believe it was because He was moved by their sadness.

What does that mean for you? It means God grieves with you over the hurts you have experienced. He is moved to tears by your heartbreak. He is neither callous nor uncaring. He is deeply involved and interested in your life, hurts, and story.

How can we apply these truths?

Knowing that God cares about your story makes it easier to come to Him. Take a moment and do what Martha and Mary did when they heard Jesus had come. They ran to Him and told Him what was on their heart. They wondered why He let it happen; they cried out in their sadness. Don't hold back your real feelings. God wants you to be honest as you call out. After all, He already knows what you've been feeling anyway. Talk to Him, and know that He hears you not only with His head but also with His heart.

_____

_____

_____

_____

_____

_____

Your love letter

It seems confusing, doesn't it? If God could protect us from the bad things, why doesn't He? And if He could save us from things that bring us to tears, why wouldn't He do that, instead of crying with us after the fact?

We need to look at a few things to help answer those questions. The first is that we never know what lies around the corner. His ways are higher than our own—He knows things we don't know yet (Isaiah 55:8–9). Jesus had plans to raise Lazarus from the dead. So even as He grieved, He knew there was hope. This is where we can go straight to God's love letter and celebrate Romans 8:28: "And we know that in all things God works for the good of those who love him, who have been called according to his purpose."

As you seek and know and love God, He will use every broken piece of your story to bring hope and life. He is the master artist; He will take the hurt and create a masterpiece. It's what He loves to do.

If you're anything like me, those words may not offer much comfort in the middle of your pain. After all, the pain is still there. And the consequences may be looming in front of you, threatening to last a lifetime. The same was so for Tamar, the woman described at the beginning of this chapter. The Bible says that she lived as a desolate woman in her brother Absalom's home. We know that at that time, a woman who had been raped was considered unmarriageable, except by the person who raped her. So when her brother raped her, he ruined her chances for marriage to anyone else. When he had her put out, he refused even to take responsibility for his actions—she was put out like she was garbage. Her brother Absalom took her in out of kindness, and she lived in his household.

We don't know what the rest of Tamar's life was like, but it seems that she stayed in that place of hurt. But what if she didn't? What if there was more to the story? What if Tamar took Absalom's kindness (of opening his home) and accepted that as God's kindness through him? Yes, life had thrown her an unexpected and heartbreaking turn, and that merited a season of sadness and grief. But Tamar didn't have to stay in that place, and neither do you or I. Even though what has happened in our pasts has ongoing consequences in our lives, that doesn't mean God can't create a new future for us. I know our God; we don't have to stay stuck. We have a hope. We have a future. As we do our part of uncovering the hurts and bringing them to Him, He is able to bring hope and life and a future beyond our imagination.

Maybe you can see and accept that, but you still struggle with why God allowed the betrayals you've experienced. Let's look at the choice God gives to each one of us: "I have set before you life and death, blessings and curses. Now choose life, so that you and your children may live" (Deuteronomy 30:19).

What does that mean to us? It means we have a choice . . . as do our parents, siblings, friends, and anyone else we encounter. Those choices impact our lives, for the good or for the bad. And when something bad happens to us, we can choose to let it drag us toward death, to let it kill part of us and destroy our futures, or we can fight towards life. God shows us the way to life, and He wants us to strive forward with everything we have.

God can bring good from every situation. We need to slowly take steps to accept where our story has taken us, so God can start rebuilding our future. We do that by letting ourselves be sad for the losses and by beginning to believe that God might have something more. It's a process; let's start today. Ask God to make these Scriptures real in your life. Let's look at them again.

"And we know that in all things God works for the good of those who love him, who have been called according to his purpose."
—Romans 8:28

"I have set before you life and death, blessings and curses. Now choose life, so that you and your children may live."
—Deuteronomy 30:19

Think of the parts of your story as you wrote about them in the last two chapters, and write in the space below how you would like to begin applying these Scriptures to your life today.

_____

_____

_____

_____

_____

_____

Journal time

In the coming days, make journal entries regarding the following Scriptures. What are these verses saying to your heart about God's heart to grieve with you, comfort you, and heal you?

> "Go back and tell Hezekiah, the leader of my people, 'This is what the Lord, the God of your father David, says: I have heard your prayer and seen your tears; I will heal you.'"
> —2 Kings 20:5

Psalm 30:5

Psalm 34:8

Deuteronomy 33:27

Isaiah 49:13

WEEK FOUR

FORGIVING OTHERS

Kitty couldn't sleep. Again, the nightmares had over-taken her in the dark. It all seemed so real—the soldiers, the smells, the fear, and the despair. It had been so long since all that happened. Why did she keep dreaming about it now, as a mother of five?

Kitty was only six years old when she was placed in a concentration camp. For four years, she was there—scared, lonely, and hungry. When the war was finally over and she was ten years old, Kitty determined never to think of that time again. She pushed the starvation, torture, and heartbreak to the back of her mind.

Yet the pain kept coming back—and it didn't seem to be going anywhere. At first, Kitty tried to ignore the sleepless nights and the fear that crept in through the day. But that tactic wasn't working. It was not until depression threatened to take over every waking moment that Kitty knew that she needed help.

Ultimately, she was hospitalized, and with the help of trained counselors, she realized it was time to remember and deal with her past. And she did. She remembered the cruelty, the sadness, and the devastation. She felt the anger and cried for the loss of her childhood years.

Kitty already believed in God and knew the Scriptures talked about forgiveness, but how could she forgive people who had robbed her of so much? It seemed impossible. But then, over time, Kitty came to realize how much her anger continued to rob her. It seemed like every day was wrapped up in thoughts of what happened. She asked for God's help.

She says, "First I had to forgive a hundred times a day, every time the thought of them came to mind. Then it was fifty times a day. Finally, it was once or twice a day. Every time they came to mind and the anger returned, I would say, "I've forgiven this.""

Today, Kitty is free. The thoughts that returned day after day disappeared over time. Now she doesn't think them at all. *She is free.*

What do you think?

Can you imagine forgiving those who hurt you—the villains that you wrote about in week two? Whether you experienced a childhood loss or a recent betrayal, how do you feel about choosing to forgive? Write your feelings.

_____

_____

_____

When you hold on to anger and can't let it go, the anger ends up robbing you of a joyful future. Does that make sense to you? Have you seen this in your own life? Write about it.

_____

_____

_____

What is your greatest fear when it comes to forgiving the person (or people) who hurt you?

_____

_____

_____

Let's read the Bible.

"Bear with each other and forgive whatever grievances you may have against one another. Forgive as the Lord forgave you."
—Colossians 3:13

"Therefore, the kingdom of heaven is like a king who wanted to settle accounts with his servants. As he began the settlement, a man who owed him ten thousand talents was brought to him. Since he was not able to pay, the master ordered that he and his wife and his children and all that he had be sold to repay the debt. The servant fell on his knees before him. 'Be patient with me,' he begged, 'and I will pay back everything.' The servant's master took pity on him, canceled the debt and let him go.

"But when that servant went out, he found one of his fellow servants who owed him a hundred denarii. He grabbed him and began to choke him. 'Pay back what you owe me!' he demanded. His fellow servant fell to his knees and begged him, 'Be patient with me, and I will pay you back.' But he refused. Instead, he went off and had the man thrown into prison until he could pay the debt."

—Matthew 18:23–30

What do these verses mean for us?

I want you to think back to the chapter in which we uncovered your story. We talked about the heroes and the villains of your journey. We will talk about the heroes in another chapter, but in this chapter, we need to look at the villains. We are called to forgive the people who hurt us. The reason we are called to forgive is because we ourselves have been forgiven. When Jesus becomes Lord of our lives, he commands us to become forgivers. And no matter what anyone has done to us, it pales in comparison to the things Jesus suffered because of all of our sin.

If we reflect—just think through our story—the fact remains that Scripture is true: We all have sinned and fallen way short (Romans 3:23). Consider this: If circumstances in your life were the same as those in the lives of the persons who hurt you, you may have made the same decisions they did, hurting others.

Think about how Jesus handled hurt. He was beaten, humiliated, spat on, abandoned by family and friends, and ultimately murdered. Yet on the cross, He said, "Father, forgive them, for they do not know what they are doing" (Luke 23:34). He was innocent, and a grand injustice was being done. He had every right, if any of us do, to call down legions of angels to rescue Him and take care of those evildoers. But He didn't. He forgave. He asks the same of us.

I know this is such a hard truth, and honestly, I find myself wanting to soften it. But there are other reasons God calls us to forgive. One, we have been forgiven. Two, He is still in charge. I take great comfort in the fact that our God is sovereign and mighty—that if the folks who willfully hurt me never address those things with God, He will take care of it on my behalf. Choices always have consequences. Our extension of forgiveness doesn't take away the consequences the persons who hurt us will have to face. (Of course, this truth also keeps me coming clean before God on a daily basis for my own choices.)

Thirdly, we must forgive because that action releases us to live. Lack of forgiveness is like a heavy ball and chain around our neck. Thoughts of revenge, self-pity, and anger weigh us down. When that is the case, God can't use our story; He can't take our past and bring a bright future if we stay bound by that ball and chain.

How can we apply these truths?

OK, so maybe you think it's time to forgive, but you wonder what forgiveness looks like—you wonder how it is done. Do you just bow your head, say "I forgive," and move on into joy and peace? Not usually. Forgiveness is a process. Remember the story at the beginning of this chapter? That's actually my mother's story. When it came to forgiving the soldiers who imprisoned her in Indonesia, it took time. She chose to forgive, but she had to remind herself of that as the anger kept coming up over and over again. "I've forgiven this," she would say when those feelings erupted. She had to "take captive every thought" (2 Corinthians 10:5). Every time she would start to dwell on it again, she would catch herself. Over time, the thoughts and anger stopped coming.

I don't know your situation, but it could be that, unlike my mom, you still have to deal with the person you have to forgive. You may wonder if forgiveness means that you have to feel warm and fuzzy toward that person in order to restore a perfect relationship. That is not what forgiveness means. It does *not* mean all is well and that you should put yourself into a dangerous relationship again. What it means is that the person who hurt you no longer has to make it right. They are free from the debt they owe you. It does not mean you should open the door to abuse, betrayal, and deception all over again. You are wise to protect yourself from destructive relationships. You can forgive, but that does not mean you should put yourself in the same position again to be harmed. I want to encourage you on this point. If you struggle with a destructive relationship, especially if it involves a spouse or family member, get some outside help to deal with the relationship. Check out Christian counselors in your area. They can help you in taking those next steps.

Let's get back to forgiveness. We know it is a process, and it doesn't mean perfect relationship is restored. It does mean that you set someone free from the debt they owe you. Now, this may be where some of you get stuck, thinking, *I can't forgive. That would make what they did OK, and it wasn't OK!* You are right; it wasn't OK. You have every right to be angry. But the beauty of it is . . . so does God. He has every right to be angry. He has every right to push us away, to give up, and to stop loving us . . . but He doesn't. Jesus gave up His rights to come to earth so we could know God, and He asks us to do the same.

We must remember that by forgiving, we can know the life and joy we were meant to know. God doesn't just ask us to forgive for the other person's sake. He asks us to forgive because the lack of forgiveness robs us of the abundant life He has in mind for us.

So how can you start? First, I want you to use the next few lines to ask God to help you forgive. Be honest with Him. Pour out your fears and concerns. Pour out your anger, and ask Him to help you work through it. He wants to help you. He wants to equip you. He wants you to be free. Write to Him.

_____

_____

_____

_____

Second, consider writing a letter to the person you need to forgive. Sometimes it helps to get all of your emotions out—to put them into words. You do not necessarily have to send this letter. Just write to the person you need to forgive, get out your anger (don't edit yourself, just get it out), and then write your forgiveness. By writing out your emotions, you have the opportunity to work through them. Even if the letter is never sent, the process helps.

If you are not big on writing, it might be a good idea to ask a friend for help. Get your feelings out with your friend in a safe environment. Talk about what happened and work through your feelings. Ask that friend to pray with you as you forgive.

Finally, you may wonder if you need to let the person know you've forgiven him or her. My opinion is that you do not need to let that person know. If that person has asked for forgiveness, yes, let him or her know. If not, you don't have to go there. My assumption is if you are still in a relationship with that person, forgiveness will be evident in your behavior, and if the two of you are not still in a relationship (or if you're in a destructive relationship), there's not much point in stirring it up—your forgiveness is more for you than for that person anyway. I would encourage you, though, to talk with a trusted friend or counselor regarding your particular situation. Pray about it. God will direct your steps.

Would you rather write a letter or talk with a friend about forgiving persons who have hurt you? Take the space below to write a plan of action.

_____

_____

_____

_____

Your love letter

Forgiveness provides such freedom—such hope in releasing all that anger! For some of you, that anger has defined you for a long time. You almost can't imagine what life would be like if you weren't constantly thinking about the past and what you experienced. You have become accustomed to thinking of yourself in terms of what has been done *to you*, rather than what has been done *for you* through Jesus. As we dig into God's love letter, the truth is there. Jesus gave everything for you. He gave His life for you to know freedom. He gave His everything so that you don't have to live in bondage any more. Don't miss it—accept that freedom.

Take a look at some more verses:

"The LORD will fight for you; you need only to be still."
—Exodus 14:14

"If you, O LORD, kept a record of sins,
    O Lord, who could stand?
But with you there is forgiveness."
—Psalm 130:3–4

What do these two Scriptures mean to you as you think about forgiveness? Write it out in the space below. Be specific.

_____

_____

_____

Journal time

Read the following Scriptures. Over the next week, make journal entries that describe what God might be saying to your heart about you, about those who have hurt you, and about your next steps. God loves you. His Word is living and active; you can rely on what it says.

"The LORD is compassionate and gracious,
    slow to anger, abounding in love.
He will not always accuse,
    nor will he harbor his anger forever;
he does not treat us as our sins deserve
    or repay us according to our iniquities.
For as high as the heavens are above the earth,
    so great is his love for those who fear him;
as far as the east is from the west,
    so far has he removed our transgressions
        from us."
—Psalm 103:8–12

Matthew 6:14

Ephesians 5:1–2

Luke 7:47

Psalm 25:4–7

WEEK FIVE

FORGIVING YOURSELF

Andrea slumped down in her chair. She wasn't sure what to do with the feelings welling up inside her heart. It always seemed to come to this. She would take two steps forward and three steps back. She would begin making better choices and then fall flat on her face. It wasn't that she couldn't make better decisions—she knew she could. It was almost as though she didn't think she deserved to be better.

What's that about? She thought to herself.

Punishment. Andrea drew a quick breath. That was it! She was punishing herself. Every time she felt a little hope, every time she began to imagine God loved her and might have a future for her that would be different from her past, she sabotaged it.

That's because I don't deserve a future, she thought as she slumped even further in her chair.

Andrea settled on that thought for a minute. She *didn't* deserve a future; that much she knew. She, better than anyone, knew the broken pieces of her story, the people she hurt, and the things she did. Why would God bring good things into her life? Why should she be allowed to know joy? Wasn't she supposed to deal with this stuff for the rest of her life? Wasn't she supposed to carry the weight of her past on her shoulders until she drew her final breath? That seemed fair and just. Others could be forgiven, but she didn't know if she could forgive herself.

Yes. It was better to just cut off hope before it was taken from her—better to save God the trouble by sabotaging her own steps forward.

What do you think?

Can you relate to Andrea? If so, write about your feelings.

_____

_____

_____

_____

Sometimes the worst villain of our story looks us in the mirror every morning. Do you find that to be true? Are you especially hard on yourself? If so, why do you think that is?

_____

_____

Let's read the Bible.

"'For I know the plans I have for you,' declares the LORD, 'plans to prosper you and not to harm you, plans to give you hope and a future.'"
—Jeremiah 29:11

"If it is possible, as far as it depends on you, live at peace with everyone."
—Romans 12:18

What do these verses mean for us?

God has a hope and a future for you. Maybe it is easier for you to see how God has a hope and future for other people. But for you? That's harder for you to imagine. Oh friend, I had a tough time with this. I couldn't imagine that I deserved happiness, so anytime God brought good things my way, I sabotaged them. I avoided relationships I knew were good for me. I shook my head at compliments people gave me. In fact, I actually thought there was something wrong with the people who believed in me; I figured they just weren't seeing things clearly. There was something wrong if they saw good in me.

The truth is I didn't deserve the good things God had in store for me. But that's another aspect of the beauty of our God. He had a hope and a future for me anyway! Not because of what I had done to deserve it, but *because of who He is*. He gives life. It's what He does. And we bring Him joy when we receive it.

That's what changed everything for me. I realized I wasn't doing God any favors by beating myself up. It finally hit me that God wanted me to know joy, accept His forgiveness, forgive myself, and live fully— because that would show other people what *He* can do! It finally registered that by living a grumpy life, without any hope or joy, I wasn't helping God or anyone else. It was the very fact that I had been broken and now knew joy that would draw people closer to God!

When that finally "took," amazing things began to happen. God had a hope and a future for me! He didn't want me focused on the sins of yesterday when He had the hope for today at my doorstep. And so it is with you. Oh, He has so much for you! Yes, we need to look at our past to understand our story, to confess, and to make it right (to the best of our ability) if we've hurt someone. But then, we need to forget the past in terms of our own failures. God has forgiven us; we need to forgive ourselves. We do no one any good by sabotaging our future. On the flip side, we do lots of folks good by accepting what He has given and living a full and rich life! We then become contagious... joyfully contagious. That draws other people to His heart, which is exactly what we are called to do, and exactly what will bring the greatest honor to Him and joy to our own hearts and lives.

How can we apply these truths?

If you struggle with forgiving yourself, it may take a little time to break free from the habit of beating yourself up. To start, it's important to make it right where you can. If you've hurt someone, try to make it right. You can write that person a letter, sit down with them over coffee, or call them and apologize for choices you've made. Doing so doesn't mean they will receive your apology, but that's not your responsibility. Romans 12:18 says, "as far as it depends on you, live at peace with everyone." You can only do your part. Take a moment to write a prayer in the space below. Ask God to show you whether you need to apologize to anyone.

_____

_____

_____

_____

If certain persons came to mind right away, write down their names and the steps you will take to apologize. Be specific and give yourself a timeline.

_____

_____

_____

_____

Ask someone in your small group or in your circle of friends to pray with you and help encourage you in this effort. It may be difficult, but you will experience such joy and freedom on the other side. You can do this.

A Woman With a Past, A God With a Future

Unfortunately, there may be some situations that you can't make right. The person may be long gone from your life, and you don't know where that person is now. Maybe the person has passed away, and you carry the guilt of not having set things straight. Whatever the case may be, if you can't make it right, *you have to let it go.* Nothing can be done, so just bring your broken heart to God, ask His forgiveness, and receive what He offers. Unfortunately, that's not usually a one-time thing. If you've been beating yourself up for years, it will take some time to really live in the freedom He has for you. To make it happen, it will take a conscious effort to listen to your thoughts and then actively change them. You will need God's help. Write another prayer in the lines below. Ask God for help in catching and changing those thoughts. He will.

_____

_____

_____

_____

_____

Another activity that might help you in this process of forgiving yourself is to give God the glass ceiling in your life. Let me explain what I mean. For a long time, I lived like I had a glass ceiling a few inches above my head. I never allowed myself too much success, too much joy, or too much hope. I had that ceiling in place to help God out—to make sure I was properly punished for all I had done.

One Christmas, after realizing the truths I've shared with you in this chapter, I actually wrapped up a piece of glass and put it under the Christmas tree. I put the name "Jesus" on the package. It was the last package to be opened, and my brother was the one who opened it. Everyone looked at me curiously until I explained what I was doing. "I'm done sabotaging my future," I told them. "I'm done with the glass ceiling. Whatever doors God opens for me, I will walk through them. Whatever joy He has, I'm taking it. I'm done fighting myself, and I'm done fighting His goodness." And that's where I am—I have walked through every open door, savored His gifts, and lived out the joy. Not always perfectly. . . and I'm still growing . . . but it has been such a beautiful road.

I can't even begin to describe what a difference giving up the glass ceiling has made! I want whatever He has—knowing full well I don't deserve it, but also knowing He loves to give it anyway. How I long for you to know that joy!

May you discover and know the same hope for your future. Are you ready to give God the glass ceiling on your life? Tell Him so in the space below.

_____

_____

_____

_____

_____

Your love letter

Here are a few more Scriptures to encourage you on this path. Read through them, and then write what they mean specifically to your life today.

> "As far as the east is from the west, so far has he removed our transgressions from us."
> —Psalm 103:12

> "Satisfy us in the morning with your unfailing love, that we may sing for joy and be glad all of our days."
>
> —Psalm 90:14

Think about these two verses from the Psalms. How far does He remove our sins from us, and what is available to us each and every morning? Write your answers below. Write how these very Scriptures can impact your day today.

_____

_____

_____

_____

_____

_____

_____

Journal time

Throughout the coming week, make entries in your journal to describe what these Scriptures mean for you.

> "Because of the LORD's great love we are not consumed, for his compassions never fail. They are new every morning; great is your faithfulness."
> —Lamentations 3:22–23

Isaiah 1:18

Psalm 51:17

1 John 1:9

Psalm 30:11–12

WEEK SIX

KNOWING GOD

Taylor was struggling. She understood she needed to uncover her story, work through forgiveness, and stop beating up on herself. Those issues weren't really the problem for her. In fact, those truths weren't much different from some of the things she'd learned in counseling. The issue Taylor could not seem to work through was the way she felt about God. She just felt . . . distant.

Other people seemed to know God, love Him, and have relationship with Him. While Taylor believed there was a God, she was struggling with understanding and knowing Him. It seemed lots of different versions of God were floating around. The God one of her friends believed in was the mean taskmaster; He was all about the rules. If you were good, He was good, but if you were bad, He would throw you away. The God that friend presented wasn't interested in helping people with their past; He just wanted them to get over it and live for Him. Taylor's other friend believed in a God who was some big loving wimp in the sky, not taking a stand for anything, just loving everyone and everything. That God made Taylor uncomfortable. How could she trust a wimpy God with her life and story?

The tough part about Taylor's confusion was that she wasn't sure what to do with her feelings. It is not like she could sit down with God at a coffee shop and have Him tell her, in detail, who He is and what He's really like. She wanted to know Him for who He really was, but she didn't have a clue how to really dig deeper. . . or whether she even had the right to ask for better understanding.

What do you think?

Can you relate to Taylor? Explain.

_____

_____

_____

_____

_____

_____

_____

_____

Do you feel like you have an accurate picture of who God is? Why or why not?

_____

_____

_____

Would you like to know God better? Do you think it is possible? What feelings come up as you think about seeking Him?

_____

_____

_____

_____

Let's read the Bible.

"In the beginning was the Word, and the Word was with God, and the Word was God."

"The Word became flesh and made his dwelling among us. We have seen his glory, the glory of the One and Only, who came from the Father, full of grace and truth."

—John 1:1, 14

> "Let us not give up meeting together, as some are in the habit of doing, but let us encourage one another."
> —Hebrews 10:25

> "He who walks with the wise grows wise."
> —Proverbs 13:20

What do these verses mean for us?

God is real. Jesus Christ is real. The Holy Spirit is real. The three-in-one God, known as the Trinity, is real. God is good. He is compassionate. He cares deeply for you. He has a future for you. He wants all of you—not just the cleaned-up parts, but all the broken pieces. He is trustworthy. He is powerful, holy, and pure. He bends His ear to your prayers. He heals the brokenhearted. He cares about the fatherless. He is mighty, majestic, and beautiful. He is love.

How do I know these things? I learned them in two ways: through His Word and through His people. And you can learn about Him in the same ways. Let's look at those two ways of getting to know who God is.

Scripture says that Jesus is the Word. If we want to know about Him, we need to dig into the other Word—the Bible. Everything you ever needed to know about God is in those pages. A lot of people will choose to read books about the Bible, and they will go through Bible studies like this one. These are good things to do; it is good to know what other people have learned. But do you know what? God has something for *you* in the Bible. He has messages for you—truth that will hit you right where you need it. Comfort, strength, hope, and wisdom—they all are there, all in those pages, all at your fingertips. If you want to know God—who He really is—read the Bible.

Second, God teaches us through His people. Do you remember back in the second chapter when we were unfolding your story, I asked you about the villains in your story, but I also asked you about your heroes—people who believed in you and showed you God's heart? People can show us God. I have a list of folks who have been God's hands and feet to me. Some brought over Christmas gifts when I was living in poverty as a single mom. Some smiled warmly when I felt like an outcast. Some Christians invited me over for a meal or loved me even though I was messy to love. You have people like them in your life, too. It might take you a moment to think of them (it is always easier to think of those who hurt us than those who helped us), but they exist—messengers God sent to remind you He's here, He cares, and He is waiting for you. That is why God wants us to spend time together, to "not give up meeting together"— because then we have the opportunity to see God's eyes in the warmth of a friend's gaze and feel His touch in the warm hug of someone we love.

Let's go further in that verse from Hebrews: "Let us not give up meeting together, as some are in the habit of doing." What does that mean? Getting together with people requires some effort. Sometimes we stop doing it because it doesn't fit into our schedule, things get uncomfortable, or someone hurts our feelings. God is reminding us to push through and keep getting together. Then we will have the chance to encourage and be encouraged.

How can we apply these truths?

As we continue along this path of uncovering our past, forgiving, healing, and letting God use us, it is very, very important that we know God. We need to know He is good, kind, and faithful. We need to know He is all-powerful. Otherwise our journey gets confusing and misdirected as we wonder about God's motives and heart.

Let's start by applying what we have just talked about. How can we dig into His Word? One tool that might be helpful when it comes to reading Scripture is to get a Bible divided into daily readings. Then as you are reading, if you find you're hungry to know more, you can go to the whole chapter or book and dig in. Also, always invite God to speak to you as you open your Bible. Tell Him that you want to learn, and ask Him to show you His truth. That's a prayer He loves to answer! Another practice that is helpful in reading Scripture is to do so with a friend— especially a friend who has been into it for a while. It's good to be with someone who has a similar hunger and who might be able to help explain things when get you stumped.

As you think about getting into God's Word, what steps can you take to make that happen? Be specific about what you would like to do or whom you would like to ask about it.

Then we come to know God by knowing His people. This method is a little trickier, because honestly, some folks say they know God but don't reflect Him at all. How do you figure out with whom you should spend time, and who will show you the accurate character of God? First ask God to bring people into your life who will reflect Him. Then get involved in a church—look for a place that teaches from the Bible, but also lives it. In other words, the *core people* at the right place are kind and welcoming. (The reason I say core people is because you can't expect the visiting folks to be kind and welcoming. They are there to get help, just like you and me.) You don't want to select a church where the core individuals in the congregation wander around with smug looks or uptight expressions. A place where God is alive will be defined by truth wrapped up in warmth. The Bible will be taught. Once you find a place like that (and perhaps you are already there), begin reaching out to those folks with the contagious smile. Spend time with them. Learn from them. Ask them to tell you their story.

Let's take a moment now to think about the heroes of your story—the people who have already shown you God's kindness. Write down their names as you thank God for them. (It wouldn't hurt for you to send them a note if possible. I'm sure they would be thrilled to know they showed you God's heart.)

_____

_____

_____

_____

Are you currently involved with persons who show you God? Describe them.

_____

_____

_____

_____

_____

How can you take steps to be around or deepen your relationships with individuals who love Jesus? Be specific and give yourself a timeline.

_____

_____

_____

_____

_____

Your love letter

God longs to make Himself real to you. Let's look at a few verses that will give you a picture of God's character. After each verse, we'll use the tool you've been using for your journal time. Write down what it says about God, and then what that truth means for your life.

> "When he cries out to me, I will hear, for I am compassionate."
> —Exodus 22:27

What does this say about God?

_____

_____

What does this mean for your life today?

_____

_____

_____

_____

"The Lord will fulfill his purpose for me; your love, O Lord, endures forever."
—Psalm 138:8

What does this say about God?

_____

_____

_____

_____

What does this mean for your life today?

_____

_____

_____

_____

_____

> "I have come that they may have life, and have it to the full."
>
> —John 10:10 (Jesus speaking)

What does this say about God?

_____

_____

_____

_____

_____

What does this mean for your life today?

_____

_____

_____

_____

_____

Journal time

Over the next week, read the following verses and make journal entries regarding what God has to say about Himself, His people, and His Word.

> "How great is the love the Father has lavished on us, that we should be called children of God! And that is what we are!"
> —1 John 3:1

1 John 4:8

Psalm 119:105

2 Chronicles 30:9

Psalm 34:8

WEEK SEVEN

LOVING GOD

Erin couldn't believe the stories coming from Trish, the guest speaker for their women's meeting. The things Trish had done, the places she had been were scary! Her childhood had been a mess, and things grew even worse once she was on her own—lousy choice after lousy choice. Now Trish was standing at the podium and smiling as if life had truly changed. She talked about Jesus as if she knew Him. It didn't seem possible. How had she gone from addictions, heartbreak, and poverty to life and hope?

Erin wanted to know more. She waited until Trish finished speaking and then quietly pulled her aside. "You talk about being free from your past," Erin said, "but I just can't imagine it. I fight the feelings from my past every day. How do I get from where I am to where you are? What did you do to change?"

Trish looked at Erin with warmth in her eyes. "You know, I can remember saying almost the exact same thing to a traveling missionary who came through our church. There was such a light in his eyes, and he'd been through so much. I knew whatever healing he'd found, it was the real thing—and I wanted it. So I asked him how he'd done it, and I'm going to tell you the same thing he told me. Ready?"

Erin leaned in closer, eager to hear the solution.

"I fell in love," Trish said, "and it brought out the best in me."

Erin didn't get it. Fell in love? This was about romance?

Trish continued, "I tried for a long time to get better, to forget the past, to make different choices. It didn't work. I just drove myself in circles. God was part of the process, but I only let Him in as a distant observer. But then," she paused as she leaned closer, "I got to know Him. I learned about Him and grew to love Him. And as I loved Him and understood how much He loved me, things began to change. I found myself wanting to make different choices because of that love. It wasn't out of a *have to* or some spiritual obligation. I wanted to keep growing because I'd fallen in love."

Erin nodded. A divine romance. Falling in love with God. Something resonated in her heart. How she wished she could love Him like that! But could she?

A Woman With a Past, A God With a Future

What do you think?

Can you imagine falling in love with God? Share about your fears or your excitement (or both) in the space below.

_____

_____

_____

_____

_____

Have you been in love? Can you see how loving and being loved have the capacity to change us? Be specific.

_____

_____

_____

_____

_____

Let's read the Bible.

"We love because he first loved us."

—1 John 4:19

"Jesus replied: "'Love the Lord your God with all your heart and with all your soul and with all your mind." This is the first and greatest commandment.'"
—Matthew 22:37–38

"This is love for God: to obey his commands."
—1 John 5:3

"I will always obey your law,
    for ever and ever.
I will walk about in freedom,
    for I have sought out your precepts."
"[F]or I delight in your commands
    because I love them."
"The unfolding of your words gives light."
—Psalm 119:44–45, 47, 130

What do these verses mean for us?

Loving God changes us to the very core. It's a process. First, we love God as we experience His love. We love Him in response. When we realize the God of the universe, the one who put the stars in the sky and

A Woman With a Past, A God With a Future

created everything around us, loves us deeply, it takes our breath away. It is amazing to know how specific His love is for us. He knows the number of hairs on our head, the way we position our body to sleep at night, and the way we laugh when we are embarrassed. He knows every detail, and He loves us completely. When we begin to truly understand that, we can't help but love Him in return.

Loving Him in response to His love draws us closer. We begin to love God with our mind and strength as we get to know more about Him. We discover that not only does He love us, but also He is good. He has good plans for us. He is gentle, kind, wise, and holy. He is perfect. We begin to love Him for who He is, not only for what He's done in loving and saving us.

Then loving Him with all of our heart and mind gives us the strength to obey His commands and believe His promises. We obey them because we have come to love Him, and we understand His motive for giving us direction is to protect us. His motive is not to rob us of life, but is to give us life. For example, the reason He doesn't want us to lie is because deceit weighs heavy on our heart and ruins relationships. The reason He doesn't want us to have sex outside of marriage is so He can protect our hearts from the hurt that inevitably follows. As we love Him, we trust Him. We stop thinking He's out to rob us of fun, and start believing He wants to protect us from harm.

And as we love Him, dear ones, we begin to believe His promises. (This we will discuss more in the next chapter.) As we begin to believe to our very core that He is real, loving, and good, then He has the freedom to heal our past and even use it for good. By knowing, loving, and believing God, we will know joy in the process, even if the path gets a little bumpy along the way. We will be free. No matter where we have been or what we have done. Freedom and life and joy will be gifts for us to enjoy.

How can we apply,
Your love letter, and
Journal time—All in one

First, let's take a look at where you are today. On the spectrum of knowing and loving God, would you say that you know Him well and love Him deeply...or that you're on the front end, discovering Him and His love...or that you are somewhere in the middle? Explain your answer.

_____

_____

_____

_____

_____

_____

Wherever you are on this journey, there is a next step. The beautiful thing is that the more you know Him, the more you will love Him, the more you will trust Him, and the greater joy there will be on your journey. And the joy won't be a joy based on your surroundings or your past or current circumstances. It will be a joy based on relationship—on spending time with Someone who loves you and whom you love. It will change everything.

This week, we are going to combine the last three sections (How can we apply these truths?, Your love letter, and Journal time), because making this real in your life (applying it) will be all about going to the Bible, knowing Him more, and loving Him in response.

So what is the next step for you? Perhaps you need to know He loves you, so you can begin that initial response of loving Him in return. If that is the case, look up the following Scriptures, and write them out in your journal. Only make them personal—put your name into the text and let God's truth speak to you at the heart level. Let me show you what I mean.

> "As the Father has loved me, so have I loved you. Now remain in my love."
> —John 15:9 (Jesus speaking)

Making it personal: "_____ (Put your name), I love you. I love you as much as My Father in heaven loves Me. That's not a small thing! Imagine how much God the Father loves Me, His only Son. I love you that much! Don't forget it. Don't walk away. Rest in My love."

Now try the same thing with some of these next verses. Take your time and do them over the coming week. Also, investigate other verses about love, and you will discover how deeply He cares. Take a few minutes after personalizing a verse, and write a response to God. Let Him experience your love.

> "This is love: not that we loved God, but that he loved us and sent his Son as an atoning sacrifice for our sins."
> —1 John 4:10

Psalm 145:13

Psalm 139:7–10

Zephaniah 3:17

Psalm 23

Maybe you know that God loves you, but you want to go deeper. You want to love Him not only in response to His love for you but because of who He is. If that's where you are, go to the following Scriptures and write out the character traits these authors talk about. Write your own note of gratitude in the form of a letter. Let Him know, as the biblical authors did, what is so beautiful about His character.

"Shout for joy to the Lord, all the earth.

Worship the Lord with gladness;

come before him with joyful songs.

Know that the Lord is God.

It is he who made us, and we are his;

we are his people, the sheep of his pasture.

Enter his gates with thanksgiving

and his courts with praise;

give thanks to him and praise his name.

For the Lord is good and his love endures forever;

his faithfulness continues through all

generations."

—Psalm 100

1 Peter 1:3

Hebrews 13:8

Deuteronomy 10:18

Matthew 14:35–36

Maybe you are in a place where you are falling more in love with God every day, but you struggle with obeying His commands. Or maybe you wonder if He will really be able to heal your past, use you for good,

A Woman With a Past, A God With a Future

and give you a hope and a future. If that's the case, go to these verses, and write out what they mean for you.

"But because of his great love for us, God, who is rich in mercy, made us alive with Christ even when we were dead in transgressions—it is by grace you have been saved. And God raised us up with Christ and seated us with him in the heavenly realms in Christ Jesus, in order that in the coming ages he might show the incomparable riches of his grace, expressed in his kindness to us in Christ Jesus. For it is by grace you have been saved, through faith—and this not from yourselves, it is the gift of God."
—Ephesians 2:4–8

Psalm 30:5

2 Peter 3:9

Proverbs 23:18

Colossians 1:12

WEEK EIGHT

BELIEVING GOD

Oh, how she loved Him. Mary gazed at the one who had changed her entire world. She was one of the few standing there at the cross. Others had run away when things turned ugly; one of His disciples had even denied knowing Jesus altogether. Mary could not, no matter what happened. Jesus had saved her. He healed her—healed her broken pieces. She had been a mess, and He looked at her with such love and tenderness. He had received her love in return. He was her Savior. She would never leave Him, no matter what.

Some of the disciples had thought He would become king. They had thought He would come in power and make a big scene—saving all of them and showing the Roman guards a thing or two about divine royalty. Instead, Jesus allowed Himself to be captured, tortured, and then killed on the cross. Mary was heartbroken by the way things turned out...but she wouldn't abandon Him. He hadn't abandoned her, and she knew enough to know there were things going on beyond her understanding. Not only that, Jesus was the first person to find her valuable. He was the first one to look at her without disgust for her past. He healed her wounds and found her beautiful. She would never leave His side.

Heartsick over Jesus being put to death on Friday, Mary went early Sunday morning to the tomb where they had laid Him. He wasn't there. Alarmed, she reported her finding to two of the disciples, who came to the tomb, saw it was true, and left. But she, still devastated, stayed and wept by the tomb. Moments later, she saw someone she thought was the gardener. He asked her why she was crying and who she was looking for. When she answered Him, He spoke her name—Mary—and she knew He was Jesus. Her Jesus, her Lord. He had risen! And how beautiful the sound of her name was as it came from His lips!

You can read part of this story in John 20.

What do you think?

Mary Magdalene believed in Jesus. As she discovered His love for her, as she realized what an amazing, compassionate, holy man He was, she came to love Him. And her belief in Him, despite circumstances, did not waver—nor did her love. Can you relate to

Mary, or does her belief seem "too much" to you? Write your heart in the space below.

_____

_____

_____

_____

Does it surprise you that the disciples ran away when things didn't turn out as they expected? Can you relate to them? Write about it.

_____

_____

_____

_____

Let's read the Bible.

"Then Jesus told him, 'Because you have seen me, you have believed; blessed are those who have not seen and yet have believed.'"

—John 20:29

> "Therefore everyone who hears these words of mine and puts them into practice is like a wise man who built his house on the rock. The rain came down, the streams rose, and the winds blew and beat against that house; yet it did not fall, because it had its foundation on the rock."
> —Matthew 7:24–25

What do these verses mean for us?

Believing God is not easy. We have an enemy who loves to sabotage our belief that God is truly real and that He is interested in our lives. This enemy prowls through our culture, approaches us individually, and tells us that believing isn't possible. He tries to convince us that trusting an unseen God is evidence of weakness and maybe even a little on the wacky side. How wrong this enemy is!

Yes, it is sometimes difficult to believe in a real God when we look at our past or face difficult circumstances—but God's reality is everywhere! You need only look at the magnificent beauty around us, the craftsmanship evident in a baby, the evidence of Him in nature. It is actually more of a stretch to believe that we are a haphazard collection of cells than it is to believe in a divine creator! Yet our God still understands it's a struggle.

Jesus's disciples, who saw His miracles and experienced the depth of love in His eyes, still ran away when times were tough. He knows it can be even more difficult for us. But He also promises that as we choose to believe, we will be blessed, we will stand firm—He will be our Rock.

Think about Mary again. She lived out the words from these Scriptures (John 20:29 and Matthew 7:24–25). She believed. Her foundation was firm. She didn't waver when she remembered things that happened in her life or even when present circumstances (the winds and rain) battered her world. She believed because she knew Jesus and she loved Him. Our greatest strength will come from living the same truth.

Friends, as we know and love God, as we choose to believe Him, He will use our past for our good, He will bring us comfort in the present, and He will give us peace and a sure footing as we think about the future.

How can we apply these truths?

My prayer is that your heart resonates with what I just wrote. I pray that hope builds in you as you imagine resting your life on an immovable rock—that you long to know the depth of love God has for you so you can love Him in return, trust Him with your past, and believe Him for your future. But you might be struggling because you wonder what that actually looks like. Maybe you're having a tough time because you don't believe like you wish you could. You want to, but you're not sure how.

It's OK. There are things you can do to build your faith and your dependence on Him. First, there are the things we've talked about—knowing Him and loving Him, digging into His Word, getting to know His character, and coming to love who He is. Another basic is to ask Him. Ask Him to help you believe. Why don't you do that right now? Pen a prayer and ask Him for help in developing and building your belief. Be real as you tell Him where you are and how you would like to grow. I can distinctly remember a time praying and telling Him I didn't believe at all— but how I wanted to! I asked Him, "Would You show me?" And He did, beyond my expectation. He will do the same for you. Write to Him in the space below.

_____

_____

_____

Other tools can help if you are struggling with belief. Consider any of these as you continue on this journey.

First, keep a prayer journal. Talk to God. Call out to Him. Keep track of the things you ask, and make sure to document how specifically He answers. Sometimes His answer will be a clear and resounding yes, sometimes His answer will be no, sometimes He will ask us to wait, but He will always answer. Keep track of His answers, and as you see His faithfulness to respond, you will grow in your trust and belief.

Second, listen to the stories. Everyone has a story. As you come in contact with other believers, ask them what God has done in their life. Listen closely. There is nothing quite as inspiring as the real-life tale of someone who has encountered the reality of Jesus. Such stories will encourage you and build hope and anticipation for what God is going to do in and for you.

Third, write down Scripture. I wrote down Psalm 86:11 on a piece of paper and prayed it every morning. "Teach me your way, O LORD, and I will walk in your truth." It has been amazing to see how He has answered that prayer!

When you think of growing in the area of belief in God's faithfulness, what step would you like to take first? It doesn't have to be something I suggested. Feel free to come up with your own plan, but be specific.

_____

_____

_____

_____

_____

_____

_____

Your love letter

The following Scriptures that you will consider in your journaling will help as you seek to be like Mary. Remember the disciples who ran away? They came back around—and boy, did they ever! When they saw

Jesus alive after the crucifixion, their belief grew to be unshakable. In fact, they were so devoted they gave every last breath (and their lives) in order to tell other people about their Savior. The same can be true of you. Take a look at these Scriptures and daily, as you journal, ask God to build in you a belief as solid as His disciples' . . . as solid as Mary's. Your life (and your eternity) will never be the same.

Journal time

Here are your Scriptures for this week.

> "'You are my witnesses,' declares the LORD, 'and my servant whom I have chosen, so that you may know and believe me and understand that I am he. Before me no god was formed, nor will there be one after me.'"
> —Isaiah 43:10

Mark 9:23–24

Proverbs 18:15

Psalm 18:1–2

John 4:42

John 17:20

WEEK NINE

LIVING GRACE

Dayna went to her knees. Something about kneeling helped her to stay focused in her prayers. She'd had a rough day with one of her co-workers and was learning to bring things to God right away. She didn't want the bad feelings and thoughts to linger in her heart. "O Lord," she whispered. "Thank You for saving me. Thank You for helping me to look at the broken pieces in my life. Thank You for healing me. I'm struggling though. I keep fighting the desire to take control of everyone and everything. I'm sorry about that thing with Janet today. I was so frustrated when she seemed to ignore everything I told her. I know I overreacted. I'm sorry, Lord."

Dayna paused, and a slight smile danced on her lips. "You are amazing. I love knowing You hear me, and that You forgive me. I love knowing You are in control. I don't have to fix everything or everyone, including Janet. All I have to do is come to You, set my heart at Your feet, and trust that I am a work in progress. Oh Lord, I can't even begin to express how grateful I am that I don't have to be perfect. I just have to come to You with all of my imperfections, and You, in Your grace and love, give me a fresh start every day, every hour, every minute. Continue to change me, and Lord, give me the grace to see others as You see me. Help me remember we are all works in progress, so I won't be quite so hard on everyone, including myself. Thank You, Lord."

What do you think?

Can you imagine coming to the Lord as Dayna did? Is there something you'd like to bring to Him now? Go ahead and write it here. He is listening.

_____

_____

_____

_____

_____

_____

As you know and love God and gain a greater understanding of His grace toward you, can you picture yourself giving grace to others? Try to write down what that looks like to you.

Let's read the Bible.

"Not that I have already obtained all this, or have already been made perfect, but I press on to take hold of that for which Christ Jesus took hold of me. Brothers, I do not consider myself yet to have taken hold of it. But one thing I do: Forgetting what is behind and straining toward what is ahead, I press on toward the goal to win the prize for which God has called me heavenward in Christ Jesus."

—Philippians 3:12–14

"Let us draw near to God with a sincere heart in full assurance of faith, having our hearts sprinkled to cleanse us from a guilty conscience.... And let us consider how we may spur one another on toward love and good deeds."

—Hebrews 10:22, 24

> "Remember that at that time you were separate from Christ...without hope and without God in the world. But now in Christ Jesus you who once were far away have been brought near through the blood of Christ."
> —Ephesians 2:12–13

What do these verses mean for us?

Grace. What a beautiful word. Grace—unearned, undeserved favor—changes everything. As we know, love, and believe God, it becomes much easier to live in His grace. As Paul says in Philippians, grace gives us the ability to keep straining ahead. We don't get caught up and stuck in our broken pieces; we just set things before God and move forward. It's beautiful...really. Every time we bring our poor choices to God, He gives us a clean slate. There is such joy in knowing that we can run to Him, that He receives us, holds us, cleans us up, and set us back on our feet. We are on a journey, each one of us. The joy comes in "forgetting what is behind and straining toward what is ahead."

A Woman With a Past, A God With a Future

Yet, as we are called to forget what is behind in order to move forward, we also are called to remember where we have been and from what we have been rescued. In other words, we need to let go of the past when it comes to beating ourselves up or holding on to old sins, but we need to remember our past so we can celebrate what God has done and tell others. Remembering our past also gives us a better perspective when others need our grace.

Friend, God has a future for you. The enemy wants to rob you of that future and keep you from sharing God's hope with anyone else. Living grace helps you move forward into the future (as you let go of the mistakes you made), and it also equips you to share hope with others (as they experience God's grace through you and your story). As you trust that God actively forgives you, you will be able to share the same hope with others.

Imagine with me a scenario: You are having a rough day. Everything is going wrong, and it seems like you are pulling out every wrong response in the book. But you've come to understand the reality of God's love for you. You've gotten to know His character. So, as in our opening story, you run to Him, pour out your heart, ask His forgiveness, and feel His grace wash over you. Maybe a day or two later, a friend comes to you and pours out her story. She's beating herself up as she talks about a lousy choice and the pain it has brought. Because you have experienced grace yourself, you are able to point her to God's heart, look at her with love, and literally live the grace of God into her life—not making her choices OK, but making sure she knows she's OK.

What an incredible gift! That is just what God intends. As we live it, we share it, and others come to know Him, too.

How can we apply these truths?

Living grace on a daily basis means that we not only accept God's grace for our past choices, but we trust Him to forgive our current mistakes and even rest in the fact that He will meet us in the future, too. It means believing that His love will stay consistent, that we can always run to Him, and that nothing can separate us from His love. There is such safety in the knowledge that we cannot be separated from His love; it makes us less tempted to try to hide from Him when we slip up and more willing to run to Him first.

So what does it mean to live grace? How can we make it practical? When any issue comes up, talk to Him right away. In other words, the minute that angry word slips out or you find yourself straying from Him, pull yourself back, ask His forgiveness, and accept His grace.

If you are anything like me, you may be used to letting things go for a while. Maybe you make a bad choice, but instead of running to God, you hope He didn't notice, and you keep going. But then it starts bothering you, so you make another lousy choice. Then you think to yourself that the whole day is shot, so you might as well mess up for the rest of it—then start fresh in the morning. At this point, you find yourself nervous about going to God, so you hide in something else and end up in a deeper mess than ever...and so it goes until you end up in a spiraling cycle of sin that is out of control.

Oh friend, don't let that happen to you. Keep a short account. Run to God often. Soak up the grace

He offers—grace that never runs dry. Start now. Take a moment to write a prayer. Ask God and His Holy Spirit to help you in this process. Let Him know how much you desire to live grace, and ask Him to meet you as you live it out.

_____

_____

_____

_____

What about extending grace to others? As we know and love God and gain a greater understanding of His grace, we find it easier to give grace to others. How do we go about doing that? I think this happens in two ways. We show God's grace as we remember what He's done and tell others, and we show grace when we forgive people who hurt us because of their own broken pieces.

Let's look at the first way: telling others what God has done for us—in other words, bragging on God. Never be ashamed to share what He has done. Never be afraid to tell others how He has rescued you and brought you new life. Sometimes we don't like for others to know where we have been, so we clean up our story and tone down our past and our desperate need for His grace. Maybe we still struggle with certain issues, so we don't think we are in a place to share, even though He has already done some amazing things in our heart. Yet our story, even if it still feels rough around the edges, is the greatest evidence we have of the reality of God.

I used to worry about telling my story. I was afraid that if I spilled out my broken pieces, others would think less of me. But I wanted people to know what God had done each step of the way. So I began to go for it—tentatively at first, but now, with fervor. I tell people. I write to you. I speak to groups. I go wherever He asks me to go, because I've discovered that it's not my broken pieces people remember, it's His saving grace. And when they make the choice to invite Him into their lives, I get the awesome privilege of being part of something beautiful and beyond myself. There is nothing like it! I promise you. We'll talk more about this in the coming chapters, but for now, just know there is tremendous beauty in living His grace for others to see.

Second, extend His grace by living it to others in your life—usually those closest to you. When you know how much grace you have needed, it is easier to extend grace to your parents, your siblings, your spouse, or your children. I won't dig too far into this, since we devoted a whole chapter to forgiving others earlier. Just keep in mind that living grace shows people God's heart. Does someone need to receive grace from you today? Write about that situation here.

_____

_____

_____

_____

_____

Your love letter

Living grace is a process of keeping a short account in our lives (clearing the slate often by asking God's forgiveness), telling others what God has done, and offering grace when we've been hurt. God's Word is full of stories of those who ran into God's grace, let it change them, and passed it on. As you read and discover this truth in your own study time, let it encourage you to be a part of that sweet biblical legacy. For now and over this next week, let's focus on the following Scriptures that will give you tools to live grace in your world.

Journal time

"Do not let the sun go down while you are still angry."
—Ephesians 4:26

Isaiah 30:18

1 John 4:14

Romans 5:17

1 Peter 4:10

WEEK TEN

LOVING OTHERS

It was the first time Jessie really noticed her father's hands . . . beyond just trying to avoid them. They were gnarled and calloused—evidence of the hard labor he had performed most of his life. Those same hands had been a source of pain in Jessie's childhood when her daddy would lose his temper and lash out. Jessie spent much time during her teenage years barely avoiding his anger and much time during her young adult years angry for the ways he had let her down. He had mellowed with age, but as an adult, Jessie hadn't much cared. Her anger had remained; the damage had been done.

But this day, Jessie saw something different. Her dad was resting, leaning back in his favorite chair—his eyes closed, his hands in clear view. She noticed some marks: old scars. She recognized one that was from when he had built her a tree house. He had attached the ladder and then tested it himself to ensure it would be safe for her. While climbing the ladder, a rung had come loose, and he had fallen, cutting his hand. The scar remained.

Jessie had forgotten about that; her anger had clouded the good he had done.

And all those hours, she thought to herself, all those hours working at the factory—he was doing that for me, for our family.

Jessie felt the tears burn in her eyes as she looked at the man she had recently forgiven. Yes, she had managed to forgive him for the hurt, but this feeling— this unexpected tenderness in her heart—was something different. She realized she loved him. Amazing!

He opened his eyes and Jessie leaned in, "Daddy, can I get you something? Would you like something to eat?"

His look registered surprise. He could hear the kindness in her tone, and he was taken aback. She had been simply civil over the years. He had gotten used to that and even felt like he deserved the distance. But this warmth? Where did it come from?

"That would be nice," he managed to say.

Jessie leaned forward and kissed his forehead. His continued look of surprise almost made her giggle.

As Jessie went into the kitchen and prepared some food, she thought about her feelings. She had always looked at her dad in light of the many ways he had let her down. When she had thought of him, she'd always thought first of his harshness—nothing else. Yet as she came to know and love God, she made a decision to forgive him. What she did not expect was how that would open the door to love him. For the first time, she was seeing her dad as a man, a broken man, who had made some mistakes, but was still her dad. And instead of thinking of only the bad, she was able to see the good he had done as well: his provision, his comfort, the way he'd made her a tree house and fixed her dolls.

"It's a miracle," she said out loud as she glanced heavenward with a smile. "Thank You."

What do you think?

As you read Jessie's story, what feelings were stirred in you? Did her childhood relationship with her dad remind you of anyone in your life? Write about that memory below.

_____

_____

Can you imagine not only forgiving that person, but also learning how to love as Jessie did? Write your feelings.

_____

_____

_____

_____

Let's read the Bible.

"We know that we have passed from death to life, because we love our brothers."
—1 John 3:14

"Hatred stirs up dissension, but love covers over all wrongs."
—Proverbs 10:12

"A new command I give you: Love one another. As I have loved you, so you must love one another."
—John 13:34

What do these verses mean for us?

As we know and love God, we start loving people. It's an amazing process that takes place in our hearts. We don't start out loving that way. We begin our journey very much focused on ourselves. We love people based on what they do for us. We love deeply if we are deeply loved. If we are hurt, we shut down—we stop loving. That kind of response makes sense to us; it's logical. But God's ways are far deeper than human logic. Something happens when we encounter the amazing love of God. When we really understand how deeply we are loved, when we begin connecting to that love through prayer and time in His Word, we start loving other people out of the wellspring of love God has provided us. It stops becoming about what someone has done or hasn't done for us, and it becomes about who we are as people deeply loved by their Savior.

I want to pause here to discuss destructive relationships. If a relationship is destructive (by that, I mean physically or verbally abusive), a woman needs to remove herself and get help. If that is your situation, don't hesitate to call a counselor, seek out shelter in your local church, or contact a close friend for help. You can come to the point of loving someone who has been abusive, but that does not mean you must remain in contact with that person. Maintain some distance until at the very least, that person receives the significant help needed.

Let's get back to love. We are called to love as we have been loved by God. How have we been loved? Freely. Abundantly. God loves us because He is love. He pours love out whether we choose to receive it or not. As we become grounded in Him, we learn to love others the same way. We love because of who we have become in Christ, and it becomes less and less important whether someone responds in just the way we think they should.

This is where the beauty of our stories truly begins to unfold. Not only do we learn to love those who have been a part of our dark past, but also we are given opportunities to love broken people God sets in our path today and in the future. He will bring a hurting person into your day, and as you hear their story, your heart will be touched to the core. Suddenly, you will feel a love for that person that is beyond yourself—a love you know is divine. And because of that love, you will want to help, walk with them, and do what you can to ease them in their journey. We will talk specifics in the next chapter, but the reality is that as you are loved, you will love others and you will make a difference.

How can we apply these truths?

What does it look like to truly love others? It sounds good in theory, but how can we bring it to pass in our day-to-day lives? First, it's a matter of spending time with God. Wait in His presence. Read His love letter to you. Hang out with people who know and love Him. As you do that, you will have a greater wellspring of love within you.

Let me give you an example that came to mind as I was walking by a lake with a spillway. When a heavy rain comes, the lake fills up and the excess water flows right over that spillway, tumbling to the rocks below. So it is with us. As we receive the love of God, as we spend time enjoying Him, worshiping Him, and hanging out with friends who love Him, we get filled up to overflowing. Then, as natural as can be, our love spills out to others.

So let's start there. What can you do to open your life to the sweet rain of God's love this week? Do you need to memorize some of His love letter? . . . spend more time singing to Him? . . . worship Him in the quiet? . . . pen some words of love? Below, write some ideas that will keep you connected with God, receiving His love (and make sure you follow through!):

_____

_____

_____

_____

_____

_____

_____

Next comes loving those who are harder to love—those who have been part of your painful stories and who may have hurt you. Invite God to help you: Ask Him to help you forgive and learn to love beyond the circumstance; ask Him to help you see the good in that person, just as Jessie was able to see the good her father had done. Pen a prayer:

A Woman With a Past, A God With a Future

Finally, in order to love others well, ask God to help you see people as He sees them. I remember praying that specific prayer one Sunday morning. When I went to church that day, one of my friends sang a special song at the end of the service. I remember looking at her and absolutely delighting in her talent. Previously, I would have heard her and wished I could sing like her, or I would have gotten distracted by a shiny button on her outfit or a hair out of place. Not this time. As I looked at her, I could feel God's love for her, and it brought me to tears. She was beautiful, gifted, and made in the image of God. Again, amazing!

I invite you to pen a prayer in the space below. Ask God to let you see people as He sees them. And then, dear one, you will naturally learn to love as He loves!

Your love letter

God's Word is full of the encouragement to love others. In fact, verses 37 and 39 of Matthew 22 say we are to love God with all our heart, soul, and mind and then we are to love our neighbor as ourselves. Loving God brings out the best in us. Something wonderful happens in our hearts as we love Him with our whole being. It changes something in us. We begin to love others so naturally that we don't even have to think about doing it. We may have previously thought of loving others in terms of what we are giving or what sacrifices we are making. Yet the beautiful thing about love is that when we give it away, it comes pouring back—not necessarily in the way we expected, but sometimes in the most delightfully unexpected ways. May it be so with you.

Journal time

In the coming days, take time to read and journal through these verses for more encouragement on loving others.

"You are the light of the world. A city on a hill cannot be hidden. Neither do people light a lamp and put it under a bowl. Instead they put it on its stand, and it gives light to everyone in the house. In the same way, let your light shine before men, that they may see your good deeds and praise your Father in heaven."
—Matthew 5:14–16

Proverbs 3:3–4

Matthew 5:43–45

Proverbs 15:17

1 Corinthians 13

Romans 13:8

WEEK ELEVEN

Ashes to Beauty

Judy was just finishing up some evening housework when the phone rang. It was Lois, a younger woman from the women's ministry. Her voice was shaky as she asked if Judy had a minute to talk.

"Of course," Judy said.

"I wanted to thank you for telling a little bit of your story the other night," Lois began. "It really touched me."

Judy thought back to Thursday evening. Her friend had asked if she would share some of her broken pieces with the other ladies in their small group. Judy had been afraid of what people might think, but even as she was kicking and screaming inside, she decided to risk it. God had healed so many things in her heart that she wanted other people to know what He had done.

"It was tough," Judy said, "but I'm glad I did it."

"Me too," Lois said, a little hesitantly. "That's why I'm calling. See, I went through something similar, and I've been afraid to tell anyone. It's eating me up inside. When you talked about all the things you felt, it was exactly what I've been going through." She paused, then continued, "Anyway, I was wondering if we could get together sometime and maybe talk through some stuff."

Judy smiled into the phone. "I would love that. How about coffee next week?"

After ironing out the details, Judy got off the phone. She couldn't believe it. A sense of joy filled her as she thought of being a listening ear to Lois. Imagine that—God would use her pain to help someone else! If He can use that mess, she thought to herself, there's no telling what He's going to do with the rest of my story!

What do you think?

Can you imagine God using your broken pieces to make a difference in another person's life? Has He already given you opportunity to do so? Explain.

_____

_____

_____

_____

_____

The enemy likes to tell us we're alone in our story. As you think about others going through situations similar to yours, knowing that you might be able to offer a listening ear, what kind of feelings does that stir in your heart? Whatever you feel is OK. If it scares you, angers you, excites you—whatever you are feeling—express it, and be specific.

_____

_____

_____

_____

_____

Let's read the Bible.

"Praise be to the God and Father of our Lord Jesus Christ, the Father of compassion and the God of all comfort, who comforts us in all our troubles, so that we can comfort those in any trouble with the comfort we ourselves have received from God."

—2 Corinthians 1:3–4

> "To bestow on them a crown of beauty instead of ashes, the oil of gladness instead of mourning, and a garment of praise instead of a spirit of despair. They will be called oaks of righteousness, a planting of the Lord for the display of his splendor."
>
> —Isaiah 61:3

What do these verses mean for us?

What beautiful verses! What hope lies in each one! The first passage, the one from 2 Corinthians, talks about how God comforts us. He meets us in the middle of our hurt and, like a loving father, scoops us up, holds us close, and give us a safe place to cry. Imagine a loving father rocking and comforting a crying toddler as he whispers, "Yes, little one. That hurt...but I'm here. I'm here." That's what our Father God does with each one of us if we go to Him.

First, we receive this sweet comfort; then we are given the incredible opportunity to be a part of someone else's road-to-healing story. God could do it alone. He could share with every one of us in a vision, through a burning bush, or in an audible voice. Instead, He lets us share with each other, encourage one another, be a part of another person's journey. Some gracious people who had been through things I had been through loved me when I was all broken. Then gradually, as God healed my heart and showed me how much more He had for me, I was able to do the same thing for others. I am getting to do it right now with you. I get to write and share the very real ways that God brings hope after hopelessness—the way He truly does bring joy after despair.

You may have been heartsick, lonely, and broken to the core. But you know, others may feel the same way—as though they are too far gone for help. But that's the beauty of our God. We are never too broken, too lost, too sad, too far away, because just as Romans 8:38 says, nothing can separate us from His love. He will pursue us until we take our last breath. He will give us every opportunity to say yes to His love and to receive the comfort He has. When we do, He replaces the ashes with beauty and the despair with hope, and then we get the privilege of being His hands and feet to others who are hurting.

How can we apply these truths?

What does it actually look like to receive His comfort? First, we need to know how to go to God when we are hurting. Options for taking your hurts to God are numerous: find a private place and talk to Him out loud, write out your thoughts on paper, or ask a friend to pray with you as you pour out your heart. It is amazing what He will do in your heart during those times. He can and will comfort you—not always taking away the hurt, but giving you the knowledge that you are not alone and that you are deeply loved.

Let's take a moment for that right now. If you are feeling particularly heavyhearted today, either talk to Him out loud or write to Him in the following lines:

_____

_____

_____

_____

The next step in applying these Scriptures is to keep an eye out for others who may be a few steps behind you in the process. Another beautiful thing about our God is that as we grow and receive healing ourselves, we will have opportunities to love others through their time of healing, too. In the previous chapter, we talked about loving others in terms of the tenderness we feel as we experience God's love. Then, as we love, we have an opportunity to invest our lives and our stories. And as we do that, joy springs up in us. We discover our purpose; we find out that not only do we need help but also we are able to offer it to someone else. Helping someone else takes the focus off of our own hurt and reminds us that there is a big picture of which we get to be a part.

As for my own experiences, it was good for me to understand and focus on my story for a while. That effort became even more worthwhile when I could use that understanding to help someone else.

Do you know of anyone who is going through circumstances similar to yours? Write that person's name, and pen a prayer asking God to help you encourage that person. If you can't think of anyone, ask God to show you someone you can encourage on this journey.

_____

_____

Your love letter

There are several reasons that God takes our broken-ness, heals us, and gives us beauty in the place of the ashes in our lives. Those reasons and His heart to do it are scattered throughout His Word. First, He loves us: He loves you; He loves me. He wants you to know the joy of a healed heart and the pleasure of sweet relationship with Him. He'll bring unexpected gifts in the process, such as allowing dreams, which you may have long forgotten, to come true. He does that because He is a good and loving Father (Romans 8:15). Every good gift comes from His hand (James 1:17). He'll delight you with surprises and splash out His love, because it brings a smile to His face to do so!

Another reason God brings healing and beauty to our lives is that He wants our lives to be like light-houses in the storm, showing other hurting people that hope can be found in Him. He wants others to know the good news, too!

Let's look at the following Scriptures to remind our hearts of this truth. Make them personal.

"He heals the brokenhearted and binds up their wounds."
—Psalm 147:3

"Is not this the kind of fasting I have chosen: to loose the chains of injustice and untie the cords of the yoke, to set the oppressed free and break every yoke? Is it not to share your food with the hungry and to provide the poor wanderer with shelter—when you see the naked, to clothe him, and not to turn away from your own flesh and blood? *Then your light will break forth like the dawn, and your healing will quickly appear.*"
—Isaiah 58:6–8 (author's emphasis)

As you read through these verses, what do they say to you about what God longs to do in your heart and how He will make that happen?

_____

_____

_____

_____

According to Scripture, as we heal and start to help others, our "healing will quickly appear." How sweet our God is!

Journal time

Let's look at some more Scriptures. Take some time over the coming week to write in your journal what the following verses mean in your life and journey.

> "Instead of their shame my people will receive a double portion, and instead of disgrace they will rejoice in their inheritance; and so they will inherit a double portion in their land, and everlasting joy will be theirs."
> —Isaiah 61:7

Jeremiah 30:17

Isaiah 58:10–11

Joel 2:25

Psalm 30:2–3

WEEK TWELVE

FREEDOM

I wanted to start this chapter with another story—a story of hope and freedom to help inspire you as you move forward. I thought of friends who have fought through the hard things and found hope in Christ. I thought of biblical heroes who loved Christ with all their being, and how that truly changed everything. But as I thought and prayed about what to share, it became clear: it was time to share my personal journey into freedom.

In the introduction to this study, I shared with you a piece of my story. I was a mess when I started this journey toward Christ and freedom. All my dreams lay shattered at my feet. My happily-ever-after marriage ended in divorce. My dreams of traveling and of being a successful writer and mother of five children were dashed as I took my job at the steak house/bar to feed and clothe my little girl. I was hungry for attention. I hurt people with my lousy choices. I wasn't honest or noble or good—or any of the things I once thought I would be.

What I didn't share was that I couldn't even lay it at anyone else's doorstep. Sure, I had my share of hurts inflicted by others, but I was the queen of my own mess. I was the one who added shame and guilt to the broken pieces, threw in a boatload of bad choices, and ended up feeling heartbroken and alone—disqualified. I didn't think I could recover from it all. It seemed like a mountain too big for me to climb. The wounds went too deep; the shame was too heavy to bear. I can remember lying in my bed and coming to a stark realization: "There is something seriously wrong with me." As much as I thought I could hide it from others, I came to the place where I couldn't hide it from myself anymore. So I had to do something...call someone...make better decisions than the ones I had been making.

Slowly, I began to seek God. It wasn't a perfect pursuit. I wasn't broken one day and whole the next. It was a journey and remains so.

But what I want you to know about is the freedom. So many times, as I worked through the hard places, I thought I would never heal. I wondered if a time of joy would ever come for me or anyone else who was in a pit like mine. I couldn't imagine my life being helpful to a single other soul. In fact, I wasn't even sure I wanted my life to make a difference—I was too focused on me. I even doubted that God is real and wondered if other people weren't just faking it. Maybe God won't rescue me after all, I thought, or maybe I'm just too broken to be rescued.

But dear one, I have the best news to share with you. God is real. He is a God of hope. Hope is real—and it's ours. Freedom is available; life is available. You can have laughter that bubbles up from that place deep inside, the kind that shakes your shoulders and brings tears to your eyes. You can find deep and abiding joy. You can find freedom from your addictions. You can have trust and comfort in your life even when the storms come. Life, real life, can be yours. You can be noble and honest and good, all the things you hoped you would be. Every bit of your story can be turned into a gift for your heart and a light for someone else's path.

I wish I could see you right now—look you in the eyes so you could see my sincerity. I have been there. And there is life on this journey. Not only life, but also future, purpose, and hope. No matter how young or how old you are, God has freedom for you: freedom to live, freedom to experience your purpose, freedom to know and love Him. No matter what your circumstances, you can have a life that is full, rich, and meaningful.

I can say that because that is what God has given me. I am a living testimony of what He can do with a heart that didn't know much, but knew to say yes to Him. He healed me. As He healed me, a very sweet thing happened: He brought some of my childhood dreams to pass. I dreamed of writing; I now get to write about the best love story ever. I dreamed of traveling; I get to travel, meet people like you, and talk about Him. I dreamed of marriage and recently had the joy of marrying my best friend. I thought those dreams were long gone, long past. God knew better. He not only had life, freedom, and relationship for me—He had even more. Like a loving father with gifts tucked behind his back, He brushed off my dreams, shined them up, wrapped them in a bow, and presented them to me in the most unexpected ways. How amazing! I wasn't forgotten. I wasn't abandoned.

I wasn't too far gone. And friend, neither are you! God is crazy about you. You are His. He is good. He wants to heal you. It's all true!

What do you think?

Can you imagine being totally free from your past, from addictions, from hurt? Have you gotten a taste of this freedom as we've gone through the study? Write your thoughts. If it turns into a prayer, allow it to flow. If you just want to journal your feelings, go there instead.

Is something or someone keeping you from the freedom God has for you? If so, take a moment and ask God to show you what your next step should be. He is ready, willing, and able to help you. Just ask Him.

Let's read the Bible.

"It is for freedom that Christ has set us free."
—Galatians 5:1

"I will walk about in freedom, for I have sought out your precepts."
—Psalm 119:45

"The Spirit of the Sovereign Lord is on me, because the Lord has anointed me to preach good news to the poor. He has sent me to bind up the brokenhearted, to proclaim freedom for the captives and release from darkness for the prisoners."
—Isaiah 61:1

What do these verses mean for us?

Providing good news for the poor, healing for the brokenhearted, freedom for the captive, release for the prisoners—that is the call, the life mission of our sweet Savior. He has good news for you. He has healing, freedom, and a future in store for you. In His precepts—as you know, love, and follow Him—there is freedom. In His death, there is life. He gave it all with you on His mind. He didn't give His life for everyone but you. He gave it for you. He longs for you to come to Him, to get to know the truth about Him, to spend time with Him, and to grow in your love for Him. As you do, He will change you from the inside out—not taking away anything that makes you uniquely you, but simply bringing His light and truth to soften the rough edges, to give you strength, to help you forgive, and to give you courage to walk away from evil.

My heart is so full right now—full of the desire and the longing for you to know what a masterpiece you are. You are beautiful—right now. You are a delight to our God. And He is faithful as the Master Artist. He will take every one of those broken pieces in your history and fashion them into a work of art. He will smooth the edges, fit them together, and, like a stained-glass window, create beauty from every color, every tint, and every hue of your unique story.

How can we apply these truths?

How can we live the freedom we've been given? It sounds good, but what does it mean on a daily basis?

How do we grasp it as our own? Three vital activities should help you get there.

First, spend time with God. I know I am repeating myself, but this is the key. As you spend time with God, everything changes. You change, circumstances change, life changes. Spend time in the Bible and in prayer. Talk to Him. Learn about Him. And don't give up. Use the tools we've talked through in the past weeks. The enemy would love to see you walk away from this journey and never know freedom. Don't listen to him. Keep going. Keep seeking. God will meet you. That's a promise.

Second, get help from wise people. I've talked about this as well. Spend time with people who know and love God. Develop friendships with people who are committed to knowing the Bible and living in freedom. Ask for specific help, prayer, and encouragement regarding your journey to freedom and joy.

Stay away from folks who leave you feeling condemned and less than enough. Some people may try to take away your trust in God's love for you; they may add a to-do list to the free gift of salvation and life. That is not truth.

On the flip side, you do want people in your life who aren't afraid to tell you the truth. If you're heading down the path toward bad choices, you want someone who will stop you in your tracks and help you make a wiser decision. So how do you know the difference between an ungodly joy robber and a godly truth teller? I would ask three questions. Does this person truly love me? Is this person grounded in God's truth? Is this person living His grace? In other words, are you hearing truth in love, or are you experiencing the grumpiness of someone who would rather not see you live out freedom? If you're ever in this scenario, ask God to show you the truth.

Third, live the freedom. I'm not sure how else to say it. Just live it. Live the freedom provided for you. If you're getting stuck in any of the issues we've talked about in this book (forgiving others or yourself, believing God, living grace, loving people), get more help, seek out resources, and ask God for direction. The bottom line remains—God has a future for you. He offers you joy and life. Sometimes that means forgotten dreams are brought back to life as He pours His blessing upon you. Other times it means joy in the midst of the mess. Life in God's freedom means comfort and peace when things go crazy; it means love when you're faced with hate and hope when you're tempted to despair. A future with God is all about a divine friendship with One who is trustworthy, kind, good, and more than enough to walk with you no matter what comes.

Freedom is yours. Live it.

In the space below, write a prayer of commitment to live in freedom. Write about what tools you plan to use to help you as you continue on this path.

_____

_____

_____

_____

_____

_____

Your love letter

The following Scriptures may help you as you continue your journey in freedom. Take them to heart. Write them down. Post them in places where you see them every day. Know this dear one—I am praying for you. Don't give up. Let the Healer in; let Him love you; let Him give you a future. And as you heal, pour yourself into others; help them know this same truth. Discovering freedom is one thing—it brings peace and joy. Introducing others to the same freedom is something else—it brings riches beyond compare.

"Arise, shine, for your light has come, and the glory of the Lord rises upon you. See, darkness covers the earth and thick darkness is over the peoples, but the Lord rises upon you and his glory appears over you. Nations will come to your light, and kings to the brightness of your dawn."
—Isaiah 60:1–3

Take a moment and write what this Scripture means for you today.

Journal time

We are at the end of our time together, but don't stop seeking. Continue going to the Bible and writing down what God is saying to you. Start with the following verses, and then keep going! He has treasures stored for you in His Word, the Bible.

> "Now the Lord is the Spirit, and where the Spirit of the Lord is, there is freedom. And we, who with unveiled faces all reflect the Lord's glory, are being transformed into his likeness with ever-increasing glory, which comes from the Lord, who is the Spirit."
>
> —2 Corinthians 3:17–18

Colossians 3:1–4

Isaiah 61:3

James 1:12

1 Peter 1:8–9

OTHER BOOKS BY THIS AUTHOR

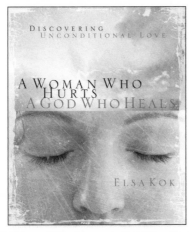

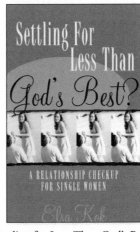

A Woman Who Hurts, A God Who Heals
Discovering Unconditional Love
ELSA KOK
ISBN 1-56309-950-0

Settling for Less Than God's Best?
A Relationship Checkup for Single Women
ELSA KOK
ISBN 1-56309-750-8

OTHER NEW HOPE BOOKS YOU MAY ENJOY

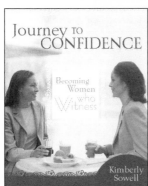

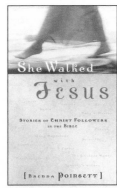

Journey to Confidence
Becoming Women Who Witness
KIMBERLY SOWELL
ISBN 1-56309-923-3

Discover the Joy
*A Collection of Devotions
for Letting Your Light Shine*
BARBARA JOINER
ISBN 1-56309-904-7

She Walked With Jesus
Stories of Christ Followers in the Bible
BRENDA POINSETT
ISBN 1-56309-830-X

Available in bookstores everywhere!
For information about these books or any New Hope products,
visit www.newhopepublishers.com.

new
hope
PUBLISHERS

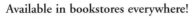

New Hope® Publishers is a division of WMU®,
an international organization that challenges Christian believers
to understand and be radically involved in God's mission.
For more information about WMU, go to www.wmu.com.
More information about New Hope books may be found
at www.newhopepublishers.com. New Hope books
may be purchased at your local bookstore.